INTROSPECTION

INTROSPECTION

LAURENCE BENAÏM

ABRAMS / NEW YORK

Iro, is an anagram of the French word for king. This is the story of two brothers who seized the opportunity to turn their name into a label, and did it in less than a decade. Their "blue note" is the street, which they observe and then idealize in their creations. Perforated leathers, vintage tweed – a supple armor in sharp contrast to the femininity of silk dresses. Designed for girls who all seem to be humming "Why do you love me?" Like Charlotte Lawrence. The Iro style has made its mark from Manhattan's Soho to Los Angeles, London, Seoul the Lebanon, Shanghai and Qingdao. A style that oozes street cred, adulated as much by millennials as their woke elders, neither Lolita nor cougar, without basis in twinism or youthism. A look much inspired by music – the foremost passion of singer-guitarist Laurent and guitarist-pianist Arik Bitton. Music in general and the music of New York City in particular. The twins have been remixing their passions and influences back since their debut in 2005. Theirs is a wardrobe fuelled by experiences, America in the Seventies, European Metal, pulsating with edgy rhythms. Iro – the instrumentals of two outsiders who landed in a universe smoothed and codified by a fashion system whose sources of inspiration they quickly came to understand. While others were content with instrumental playbacks and guitar tunes, they worked on their chord diagrams, frets, open chords and bass chords. "We learned on the job," as they say. Turning winter into summer and summer into winter, the faces of Iro would wear their shearling with bare legs. Celebrities like Anja Rubik, Aymeline Valade, Karlie Kloss and Constance Jablonski. Women who look straight down the lens, stating a character more than striking a pose. Nothing is fixed, neither the look nor the fabrics. Materials that hold together like riffs. Fleeting glimpses of new and familiar songs based on endlessly repeated chord loops. It's all about getting the tempo right every time, "striking a balance between sexiness and tomboy appeal." The casting reflects the company itself, which still today operates like a startup. Think apartment-based business with a foothold in every city, where you somehow always end up gathering in the kitchen.

Arik and Laurent Bitton vary their chord and texture modulations in line with the seasons, but never change course. "Our kind of girl likes to wear the same outfit regardless of setting or season. Two or three dresses, perf leather jacket, one pair of boots, see-through T- shirt – that's Iro in a nutshell." *Ir* from the Hebrew "to come from a city," *iro*, meaning "his city." Here, on a toll-free highway from NY to LA. "On the road again", at the heart of a world where never-ending legs serve as highly sensitive antennae.

Iro shapes attitudes as a whole. The attitudes expressed in ad campaigns and the attitudes conveyed in Iro's iconic window displays. Two-page photo spreads that come to life behind glass facades. This book marks Iro's fifteenth anniversary in 2020, presenting the spirit of an enterprise that has built brand substance while still remaining as mysterious as those three capital letters, Iro. Dark and girlie. Sun lover and creature of the night. Feminine and masculine. Inside and outside. A brand with a stripped-down graphic style that stands in sharp contrast to the twin's unbridled taste for materials. Leathers, tweeds and all those other fabrics that they have helped to debourgeoisify. Their image is inseparable from the clothing to which it gives life. A trend-driven image that encapsulates the longings and dreams of a kaleidoscopic generation.

Laurence Benaïm

//
Everything starts with a line, a figure, a way of moving, swinging the hips.
A way of being there but remaining mysterious. But not mysterious like before.
An instinctive, new kind of mysterious. Something that carries everything
along with it. Something seductive.*//*

Arik & Laurent Bitton

IMAGES

We started out alone, and now we tell stories through images.
All of Iro's campaigns correspond to particular moments in our lives.
They match up with our desires. "Iro is about living in the present
moment, one step at a time, one day at a time. One moment it's Paris –
the beauty of its dawn light and nighttime lights. The next, it's Left Bank,
Right Bank and a piano thrown out of tune by a jumble of disconnected
stories. Our campaigns tell the story of who we are, what we believe in.
They're about meetings. About everything that gets lines moving.
Looking at the world, not shutting yourself away in a world of your own.
No false reality. No guidelines either. It's about assembling a new team
every time, in the same way as you assemble a garment.
Piecing together a story where everything from A to Z comes in a zillion
shades of gray and white – from set design through hairstyling and
make-up, right down to the last little touch-up. The aim is always to create
moments, weave a tale, conjure up images based on what a model or an
actress communicates. By her presence and her personality.
We ask her to be herself underneath our clothes. Play her part.
Not try to embody a label whose brand DNA has been sequenced by
some marketing consultant. It isn't true that truth has many faces.
The truth we seek feeds on doubt and certainty, seizes the moment
as it passes by. You can't force things.//

AB+LB

HER MOOD

FALL-WINTER 2013 KARLIE KLOSS PHOTOGRAPHED BY
CLAUDIA KNOEPFEL AND STEFAN INDLEKOFER

"Concealed beneath a chunky knit is a
delicate presence. An incognito presence,
recognizable anywhere. Free, wild and
worldly-wise. The shearling aviator jacket is
a first – a first for a girl who doesn't need to
see to be seen. Even with her face hidden,
quite unintentionally, she gives herself away:
Karlie forever."

AB+LB

"This is the story of a rigid sequin that became softer than a leather glove with repeated washing.
A sequin that had lost its sparkle but was then revived by a body in motion – regained its glossy roundness,
found it could bend again, thanks to movement. Tailored jackets that invite perforation like jeans;
big eighties shoulders and tight-fitting clothing: this is an attitude that reworks yesterday's style, gives it a natural vibe.
For us that also meant moving toward the "urban living lab concept" – creativity in an urban context."

AB+LB

STONEWASHED SEQUINS

FALL-WINTER 2010 ENIKO MIHALIK PHOTOGRAPHED BY KARIM SADLI

SILVER
WHITE

SPRING-SUMMER 2014 KATI NESCHER PHOTOGRAPHED BY
CLAUDIA KNOEPFEL AND STEFAN INDLEKOFER

"Neither minimalist, nor spectral,
a white like some black that lets itself
be devoured, punctured and makes
light of everything. At Iro we strike
an attitude – one to match the girl in
the spotlight. Neither changed nor
overdone, simply revealed in all her
beauty. Stolen moments recomposed
in an image."

AB+LB

"Twisted volumes and warm-you-up or cool-you-down textiles. Protection meets softness.
Extreme temperatures and the breath of life that never, ever, blows cold."

AB + LB

TRASH & WASH

FALL-WINTER 2017 SASHA PIVOVAROVA PHOTOGRAPHED BY COLLIER SCHORR

"My photography for Iro feels deeply connected
with their denim. I think real intimacy comes
from people being completely at ease with each other.
Denim can create a sense of this intimacy, and of power
for people when they wear it. This is how I see Iro."

Collier Schorr

ALL ABOUT LEGS

SPRING-SUMMER 2019
ALTYN SIMPSON
PHOTOGRAPHED BY
CHRIS COLLS

"Desaturated grays and slightly blurred
Ikat prints, the contrast between a threadbare
carpet and the best of all possible settings.
And in the center, a girl whose presence
brings it all crashing down, the luxury
of a presence in no man's office
expressed in her eyes".

AB+LB

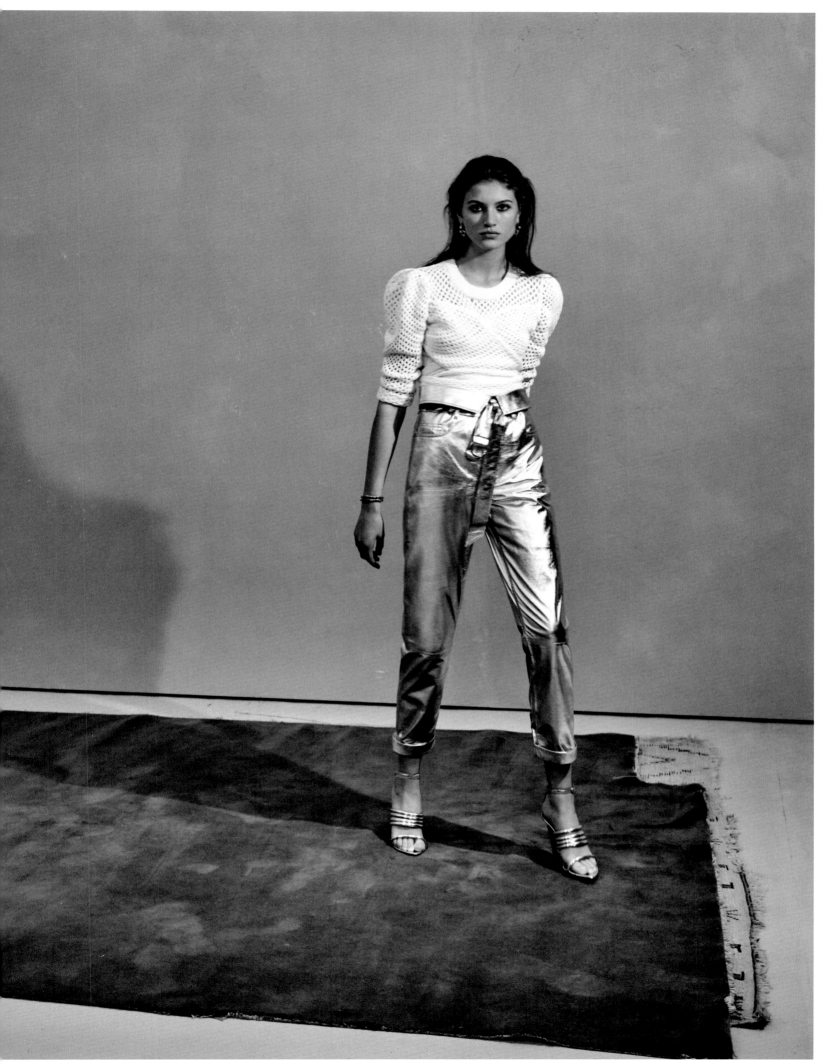

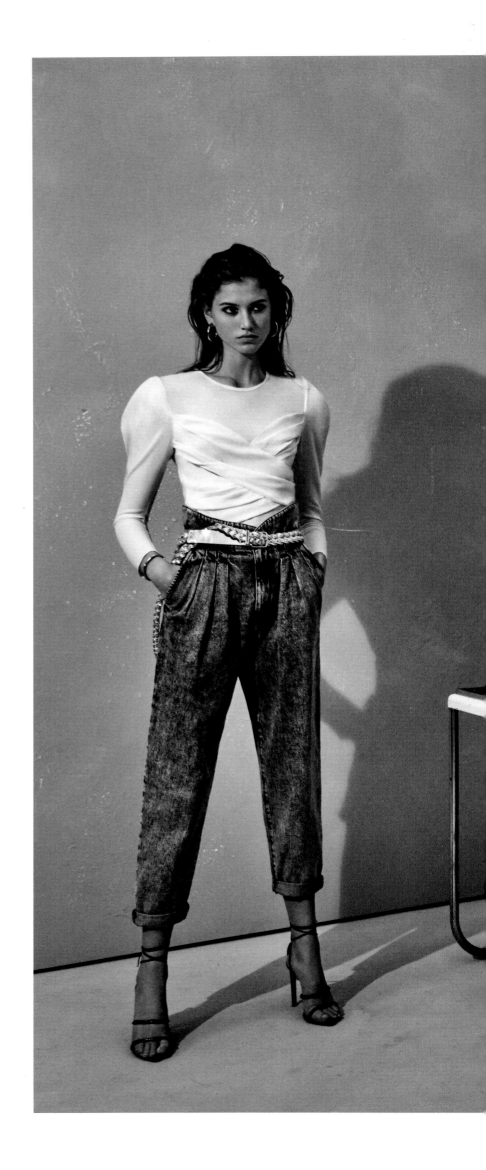

"Taylor Hill, supermodel with 13 million Instagram followers, just as she is. Wearing no make-up (or almost none) except for the odd touch of silver by way of eye shadow. Cosmetic presentation of another kind."

AB + LB

KNOWN BUT UNRECOGNIZABLE

SPRING-SUMMER 2017 TAYLOR HILL PHOTOGRAPHED BY COLLIER SCHORR

SHADES
OF WHITE

SPRING-SUMMER 2013
KASIA STRUSS
PHOTOGRAPHED BY
CLAUDIA KNOEPFEL
AND STEFAN INDLEKOFER

Iridescent white, mat white, creamy white,
sandy white … Iro road movie
Number One, leather jacket and jeans lit up
in a muted glow by the Californian sunlight,
projected shadows, let's go far away…

ZENITH

SPRING-SUMMER 2012
MAGDALENA FRACKOWIAK
PHOTOGRAPHED BY
CLAUDIA KNOEPFEL AND STEFAN INDLEKOFER

"A whole new world of possibilities opened up for us.
The images became sunnier. The blackness of New York
gave way to light and washed-out bright colors that
played a more sensual, fresher game of seduction.
We wanted to show that a girl can seem sexy
without looking like a bimbo."

AB+LB

TEXTURES

FALL-WINTER 2012 EDITA VILKEVICIUTE
PHOTOGRAPHED BY CLAUDIA KNOEPFEL
AND STEFAN INDLEKOFER

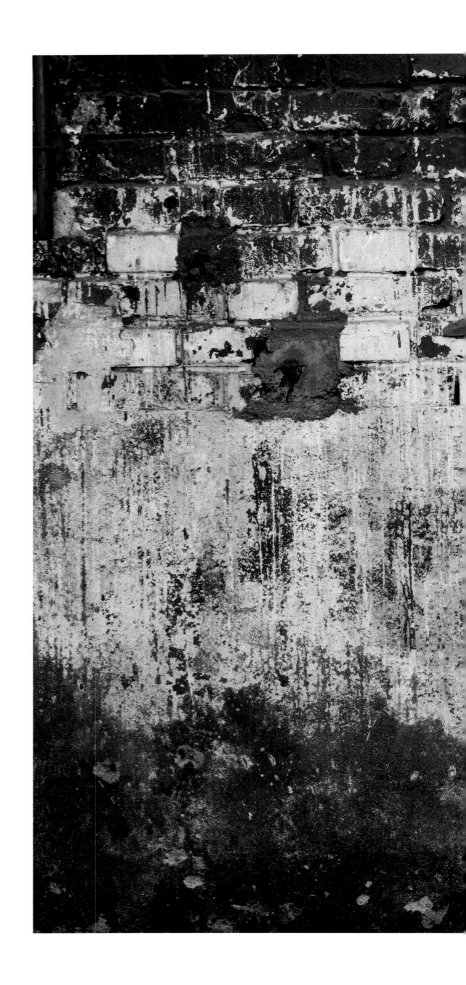

WILLIAMSBURG

FALL-WINTER 2018 LUNA BIJL
PHOTOGRAPHED BY COLLIER SCHORR

"Williamsburg: casual shearlings
that keep out the freeze. Leather
over-the-knee boots on the tarmac.
Your typical Brooklyn girl crossing
the East River with Amazonian
aplomb. Fearless.
No false modesty …"

AB+LB

INTERCEPTIONS

"Polaroids and vinyl – a movie setting
for a non-girly actress. Aymeline
pulls off a role that had us worried,
because this is never going to be
about overt girlishness. This is primarily
about line, about a construction
that begins at the shoulders.
A gesture that flows naturally
and requires no effort …"

AB+LB

SPRING-SUMMER 2015 AYMELINE VALADE PHOTOGRAPHED BY
LACHLAN BAILEY

"What matters most is self-acceptance.
Being your own kind of beautiful.
The kind that makes you unique,
singular. Doing your own thing and
creating your own style by turning your
flaws into strengths. Transcending them
without trying to look like someone else.
This is also about radiance – that feeling
of elation that comes from wellness,
being in sync with those around me,
the people I love. Real beauty isn't
self-centered. It isn't self-absorbed like
a selfie. It's a two-way conversation
that magnifies who you are.
With no trace of posturing."

Aymeline Valade

TRILOGY ATTITUDE

FALL-WINTER 2016 ANJA RUBIK PHOTOGRAPHED BY COLLIER SCHORR

" She's committed, determined. Anja is one of those women who keeps you firmly on course, makes you question all your certainties and rethink your thinking. It all started with a first capsule wardrobe ... It was a real encounter – the first of a trilogy of collections (the one and only trilogy as it happens), captured by Collier Schorr."

AB+LB

"Silver and gray diamonds in a New Jersey motel – our first jewelry line. Pure allure."

AB+LB

SOFT SKIN

FALL-WINTER 2014 **KARMEN PEDARU** PHOTOGRAPHED BY **JOSH OLINS**

DENIM US

"We were looking for your typical French beauty.
And in she came, complete with the swagger,
the allure – defiant but still a bit of a mystery.
That Certain Something that immediately marks
her out as an ambassador. Even in an undershirt
that she probably stole from her man.
Jeans, maybe just a touch of perfume.
And above all, a look. Liberated."

AB+LB

SPRING-SUMMER 2010 CONSTANCE JABLONSKI
PHOTOGRAPHED BY BENOÎT PEVERELLI

"Right from the beginning of my career,
I understood that posing naturally is all about
letting the clothes speak for themselves.
Iro works for day or evening wear.
It's an intrinsically French label.
Not in the old-fashioned sense of elegance
– the little black dress sense. But in the sense of
its brand attitude: rock-n-roll but also feminine,
with much finer textiles than before, and
that effortless *je ne sais quoi* that stands out
from the crowd."

Constance Jablonski

"Achieving an everyday style is also about
feeling good about yourself. Able to adapt to
any situation, anywhere, anytime, without
playing games but without giving too much
away either. Being there, understanding people
and always knowing your place."

Constance Jablonski

SPACE
DISCO

FALL-WINTER 2019
ABBEY LEE KERSHAW
PHOTOGRAPHED BY
CHRIS COLLS

"An abandoned loft in the Bronx
turned studio. We've lost count of
the time that has elapsed since then
… Asymmetry, craft weaving with
Lurex highlights, industrial gray
finishes and re-embroidered metal
sequins. A mix of graphics,
roots spirit, tailored design
and deconstructivism where décor
meets allure".

AB+LB

IMMERSION

NEW YORK
PARIS
STUDIO
SHOWROOM

It could be the kind of offbeat heroine you meet in a book by Joyce Carol Oates. Breezing into a small town in New York State in a pink- orange Cadillac. Or the kind played by Geena Davis and Susan Sarandon. Thelma and Louise hitting the Arkansas highways on a weekend vacation when nothing turns out right. Their shadow looms large over this chick with the devil-may-care attitude. This girl unfazed by danger, clad in her perforated leather, black fishnet top, deconstructed tuxedo pants and hoodie. Iroad movie does *The Wild One*, leaving out the switchblade and the slicked-back hair. Vacant city spaces, somewhere between the film library and the loft. A location just big enough and tangible enough to add sexiness to the iconic leather jacket. An out-of-frame jacket, built to rule. With that worn-in look of stonewashed jeans. Daylight tones, street vibe – the mood cues come thick and fast. All of them straight out of the Great American Dream but no two alike. Steinbeck's wrathful grays. The chrome surfaces of *Easy Rider*. Rocky Balboa's mispronunciations. "TV Screen" as sung by Iggy Pop and Goran Bregović's in *Arizona Dream*. It might be the red plaid flannel shirt worn by Tony Hastings (Jake Gyllenhaal) in *Nocturnal Animals*. Or a Jim Morrison shirt. Or it might be anti-pop star Billie Eilish saying she writes on her bedroom walls the things that frighten and annoy her. Things we'd rather not think about as we sing along with her to "Bad guy". No diving mask, just a white oversized T-shirt and skinny-fit jeans. It could be a whole heap of images – the umpteenth compilation of recycled memories. Everything you have ever cut and pasted. When it's actually the complete opposite. Because this moves. This has life. This is made for one thing and one thing only: to make people want to wear it. Otherwise why do so many women spend time in front of the mirror trying on high-waisted leather pants? Or those dresses that for all their flowery appeal never sink into cheesiness? It isn't one type they belong to but several. Romantic and dark. Equally at home in New York City or Paris, where graffiti couture cocks a black- penciled snoot at the gluten-free preserve of the bourgeois bohemian. "We loved the quirky rock side of Martine Sitbon, her burnout velvets. Also of course, Azzedine Alaïa, Hussein Chalayan,

Helmut Lang…" Iro caresses and Iro enfolds. One plus one makes three letters: Iro. A universe built on faults. With an office no bigger than a changing room to serve as nerve center, and for background music the mixed rhythms of "Let's Dance" and pumice stones rattling round in the washing machine. "Broken volumes … no cloning, no muse …" Words that are spoken, then settle. Staccato words that interrupt the silence like the eyelets on raw leather, fraying the edges of an expanse of snow-white cotton that seemed so peaceful until now. This is blunt talk for an extraordinary success story that is certainly one of the least ostentatious of the past decade. Unpolished language that stands in contrast to the stripped-down perfection of the boutiques, where every spotlight, every last lighting detail is minutely planned in-house. But then everything here is prompted by instinct, powered by a two-fold passion. On the one hand, a love for the architectural style of Ludwig Mies van der Rohe, Herzog & de Meuron and John Pawson. And on the other hand, a love of materials in the raw – those distressed, beaten- up, abraded finishes that are the prerogative of youth. Because the median age of Iro's 200-strong workforce (including 70 in Paris) is 30 or less – not a wrinkle in sight. "No rules. We follow our feelings. For us, summer doesn't necessarily mean azure skies and silvery sand. It's about coming up with a new urban mood every time. Iro is never about narrative. It's about identity and feelings."

Laurence Benaim

IMMERSION
NEW YORK

"New York: my fingers tickling the ivories of a Steinway piano
on the Upper East Side, with our eyes turned toward
Downtown New York. Lower Manhattan as it used to be, in the early
2000s: the stamping ground of the girl in the miniskirt in minus
10-degree weather. By day, Lower Manhattan meant Juicy Couture
and heels in a sports bag. By night, it was a dater's delight.
But something is niggling us. We want to start something of our own.
Follow in our parents' footsteps without copying them and without
betraying them either. Do our own thing. This was just after our
parents went bankrupt following a poor season caused by shoddy
manufacturing. For them, the world of music and rock music in
particular was the world of drugs and death. I was wasted but there
was someone who depended on me so I had to clean up my act.
And that's how Iro came about. Born on a knife-edge,
more grunge than preppy. In a nutshell, born with a song."

Laurent Bitton

"To return to New York is to return to a city where nothing ever stays the same and nothing disappears without a trace. Where a girl in a ball gown can be seen coming out of a garage … Where the walls, streets and facades of buildings proudly display the passage of time— that slightly worn look without which life makes no sense. That look so dear to our hearts. Trying to do Iro shoots in polite neighborhoods never works …"

AB+LB

IMMERSION

PARIS

"Paris is our city. It's where we learned the difference between beautiful and not-so-beautiful. Our perspective was shaped on the streets of New York City but it was Paris that defined our idea of taste – those fine distinctions that make the difference. But there's a sharp, hard edge to those distinctions.

Because Paris is also a city of cliques where people who don't fit in are excluded. Quickly made to feel lonely, isolated. And there is no better reflection of that isolation than the world of fashion. In the beginning they said 'If you want to exist in this business you have to do it our way.' We soon understood that we had to do the exact opposite. To exist we had to be ourselves.

So we went looking for our inner strength. The strength of our dreams – the strength behind everything we had achieved. Being pigeonholed would have suited us just fine.

It was the pigeonholes that weren't fine with it. So we did otherwise. We shaped our own destiny by striving to give concrete form to our inner world. Turn our dreams, an image, into the reality of ready-to-wear fashion for women who express themselves more through their attitude than a logo.

…

For us, luxury doesn't mean a label. It means savoir-faire, with Paris
as its time-honored capital. It's true that we always have to
complicate things. Lots of items per season (350).
Lots of different textiles. Lots of hard work simply for the sake of
keeping up with a city that is all about representation. Where
inaccessible fashion has become a pose. Where the presentation
of self verges on obsession. We have never mixed
our private lives with our brand identity but that hasn't
stopped us from giving our all to this business."

AB + LB

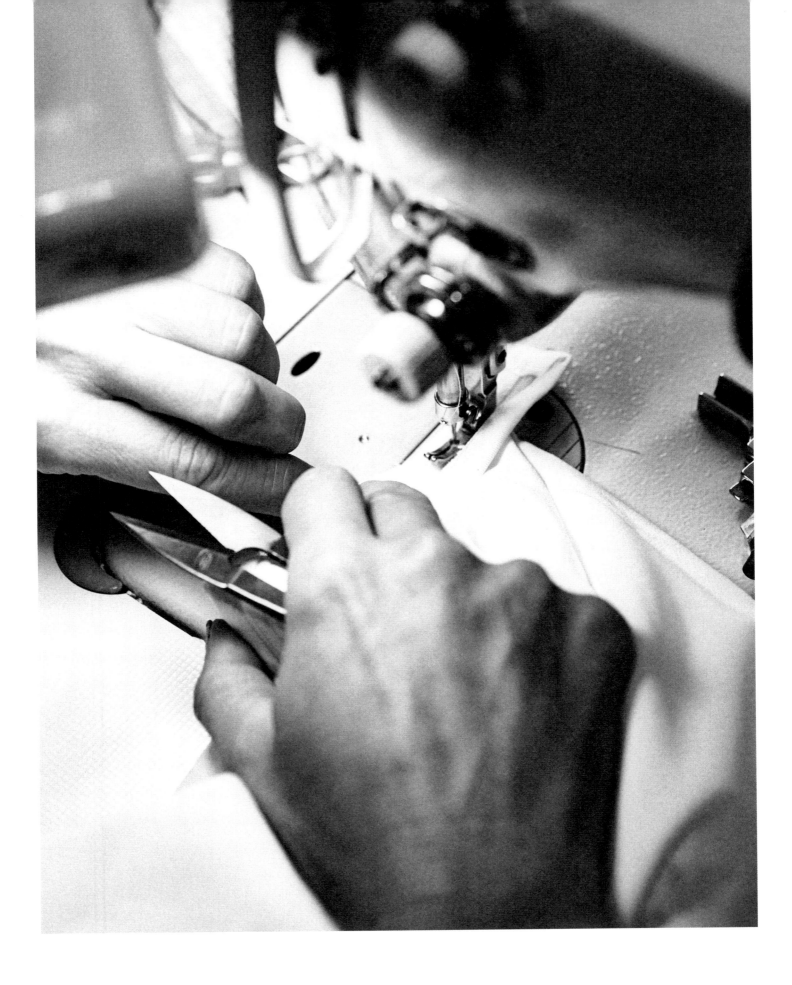

"A rather oversized sleeve … with a very short length. Buildings, finishes, materials that mark you out from the crowd. I wanted to be an architect but I had to give up my studies to work with my father. What could have been a source of frustration led me to change my whole outlook on the future. Play with lines and spaces. Whether you're dealing with a place or an item of clothing, everything starts with the foundation. It's all in the detail, in the difficulty of simplicity. We never work in two dimensions. Everything is molded then assembled to create a 3D model. So you can see it from all sides, take the guesswork out of designing. Clothes are spaces you inhabit. They have to be beautiful inside and out. This isn't about a uniform. It's about a woman moving. About searching for volume – loose but not shapeless, carefully stitched but not fussy. Structured and tailored without being stiff. Raw edges, unlined. Lots of leather. Leather pounded and hammered into shape. Gender-neutral fabrics. Draped dresses. Exclusive prints. Piercings, patches. Summer 2011 marked a move toward an increasingly hand-crafted approach. But our motto remains unchanged, ever faithful to the idea that nothing must ever feel heavy. Neither the 300 hundred rings sewn on by hand nor the effects of stone washing. We love to take luxury beyond its comfort zone, make it urban by reworking the fabrics. That was the point when middle-class girls started paying us a visit. The rest is history – a history that changes shape with every new season. Cleavage but shoulders too. Big, wraparound jackets … The reason our oversized pieces never bunch up is because they've been tested out by a fitting model. If something isn't quite right, we start again … It's a great feeling to know that you're doing this for a real audience."

A B

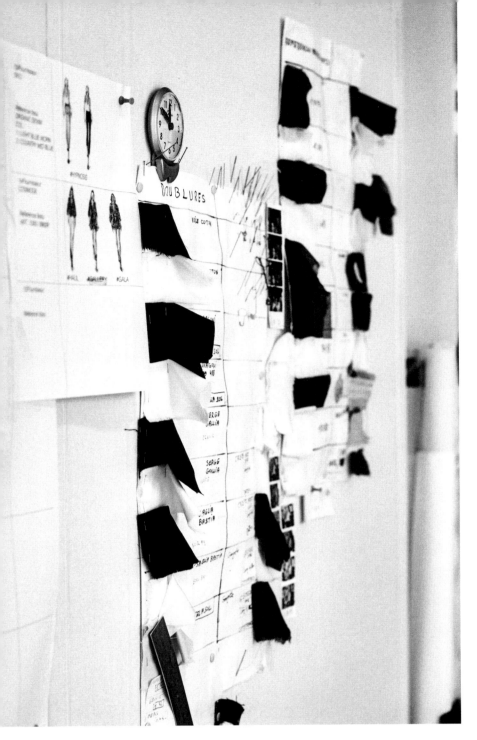

IMMERSION
SHOWROOM

Paris HQ

Neither cocoon, nor aquarium.
Under a large veranda, travertine flooring
throughout. A modular space, bathed in the daylight
that streams in through the huge glass ceiling panels.
An atmosphere softened by the muted tones of the
furnishings: Hans Wegner PP MØbler collection
white ash and blond leather chairs; and those
concrete tables where buyers lay their laptops. A soft
and lounge-like stopping place at the heart of Iro.

INVITATION

"Every Iro boutique is a three-dimensional representation of what we like and what we are – of our passion for spaciousness and light. Our meeting with the interior designer Tanju Özelgin marked the opening of the first boutique, based on an approach where the proportions, the lighting and the materials provide a divide between spaces to create an ultra pared-down aesthetic. It's a pretty radical concept. Hence our decision to combine raw concrete and wood in our rue Saint-Père store, set off by large expanses of white – immaculate expanses that almost appear to float – and Hans Wegner's Scandinavian furniture. We've always loved his soft curves and organic shapes, his fusion of function and comfort, the sense that the passage of time will bring out the wood's character. After that, the spaces evolved. We combined limestone with a beech-paneled surround with warmer tones. The idea was to break free from our clients' expectations of a boutique – create a more immersive experience. More recently, we've moved toward terrazzo flooring, combining fine aggregates with brushed aluminum panels. The finished concept has seen the introduction of 70s-inspired minimalist glass tables, with mid-century design classics such as Pierre Paulin's lounge chairs adding touches of bold color."

AB

19-DEC-2005
FRANCE
68, rue des Saints-Pères
75007 Paris

2005

2008

◀

19-DEC-2008
FRANCE
46, rue Étienne-Marcel
75002 Paris

02-JAN-2008
FRANCE
53, rue Vieille-du-Temple
75004 Paris

2012

▲

03-JAN-2012
FRANCE
38, rue Saint-Sulpice
75006 Paris

2013

02-JAN-2013
SPAIN
Calle Claudio Coello 32
28001 Madrid

03-JAN-2013
FRANCE
10, rue Royale
75008 Paris

▼

01-SEP-2013
TURKEY
Beymen Istanbul

01-OCT-2013
ITALY
Via Borgognona 29
00187 Rome

2014

▲

01-FEB-2014
USA
450 Broome Street
New York 10013
◀ (left-hand page)

01-APR-2014
FRANCE
8, rue des Archers
69002 Lyon

01-APR-2014
USA
325 N Beverly Drive
Beverly Hills CA 90210

01-JUL-2014
USA
1319 Abbot Kinney Boulevard
Venice CA 90291
▼

01-JUL-2014
FRANCE
Galeries Lafayette
40, boulevard Haussmann
75009 Paris
▲

01-AUG-2014
DENMARK
17, Østergade
1100 Copenhagen

01-AUG-2014
UK
91 Pelham Street
SW7 2NJ London

01-NOV-2014
GERMANY
Residenzstraße 26
80333 Munich

2015

06-JAN-2015
FRANCE
Le Bon Marché Rive Gauche
24, rue de Sèvres
75007 Paris

13-NOV-2015 —— 2015
CHINA
Shop LG01, Silvercord
Tsim Sha Tsui
Hong Kong

08-OCT-2015
CHINA
10 Ice House Street, Central
Hong Kong
▼

2016 —— **23-JAN-2016**
CHINA
58 Paterson Street
Causeway Bay
Hong Kong
▼

15-FEB-2016
USA
241 Columbus Avenue
New York 10023

◀ **15-MAY-2016**
USA
1013 Madison Avenue
New York 10075

15-SEP-2016
CHINA
Shop 355 & 356
The Parisian
Macao

16-SEP-2016
FRANCE
45, avenue Victor-Hugo
75016 Paris
▼

26-SEP-2016
CHINA
Shop 2224A Harbour City
Tsim Sha Tsui
Hong Kong

11-NOV-2016
CHINA
Shop LG2-02 Festival Walk
Kowloon Tong
Hong Kong

2017 ——

▲
25-JAN-2017
CHINA
Shop 203A/205, 2/F
Grand Gateway
1 Hongqiao Road
Xuhui District
Shanghai

▶
13-SEP-2017
BELGIUM
51, Huidevettersstraat
2000 Antwerp

15-SEP-2017
BELGIUM
82-84, avenue Louise
1000 Brussels

21-SEP-2017
CHINA
Shop B1007, B1/F, SKP
87 Jianguo Road
Chaoyang District
Beijing

23-SEP-2017
CHINA
Shop 306, 3/F, New Block B
Hangzhou Tower
21 Wulin Square
Hangzhou

23-OCT-2017
PORTUGAL
Avenida da Liberdade 224
1250-096 Lisbon

27-OCT-2017
FRANCE
5, rue Paradis
06000 Nice

30-AUG-2017
CHINA
Shop 328
3/F, Deji Plaza
18 Zhongshan Road
Nanjing

13-DEC-2017
CHINA
Shop 303a, 3/F
East Building
WF CENTRAL
269 Wangfujing Street
Dongcheng District
Beijing

22-DEC-2017
FRANCE
9 bis, rue Marius-Reynaud
13100 Aix-en-Provence

▲ —— 2018

14-APR-2018
USA
701 S Miami avenue #141
Miami FL 33131

20-APR-2018
CHINA
Shop 2206-1
2F, Hisense Plaza
117 Aomen Road
Shinan District
Qingdao

30-APR-2018
CHINA
Shop 309 3/F, Reel
1601 Nanjingxi Road
Jing'an District
Shanghai

16-MAY-2018
SWITZERLAND
10, rue du Perron
1204 Geneva

18-MAY-2018
CHINA
Shop UA1003, B1F
261 Changanbei Street
Beilin District
Xi'an

17-AUG-2018
CHINA
Shop 233, 2F, The Mixc
Heping District
Shenyang

14-SEP-2018
CHINA
Shop LG1-7 IFC
No.8 of Century Avenue
Pudong District
Shanghai

01-OCT-2018
ISRAËL
33 Shabazi Street
Tel Aviv

18-OCT-2018
CHINA
Shop B134+B135
K11No.300 of Huaihai
Middle Road
Huangpu District
Shanghai

14-DEC-2018
CHINA
Shop 372, The Mixc Shenzhen
No.1881, Bao'an Nan Road
Luohu District
Shenzhen

18-DEC-2018
CHINA
Shop 238, The Mixc Shenzhen Bay
No.2888 Keyuan Nan Road
Nanshan District
Shenzhen

2019 ——
02-JAN-2019
KOREA
Hyundai Busan 2F 125
Beonmil-ro Dong-gu
Busan

29-JAN-2019
CHINA
Shop 1232, Tai Koo Li
No.8 of Shamao Street
Jinjiang District
Chengdu

28-MAR-2019
CHINA
Shop IRO 2/F, Wangfujing
No.15, Zongfu Road
Jinjiang District
Chengdu

04-APR-2019
CHINE
Shop A2-4, 2/F
Wuhan International Plaza
No.690, Jiefang Boulevard
Hankou District
Wuhan

28-APR-2019
CHINA
Shop L01040-1, 1/F
Wangfujing Shopping Center
No.2, Kehua Middle Road
Wuhou District
Chengdu

19-JUL-2019
CHINA
Shop 173-2, 1/F
Coastal City Shenzhen
No.33, Wenxin Fifth Road
Nanshan District
Shenzhen

27-OCT-2019
CHINA
Shop 411a, No.1 IFS
Section 3 Hongxing Road
Chengdu

OPENED IN 2013, NEW DESIGN CONCEPT SINCE 2019 ⎯ 2019

FRANCE
Printemps
64, boulevard Haussmann
75009 Paris
▼

02-JAN-2019
KOREA
Hyundai Main B2F
165 Apgujeong-ro Gangnam-gu
Seoul

11-JAN-2019
KOREA
Hyundai Pangyo 3F
20 Pangyoyeok-ro
146 gil Bundang-gu
Seongnam-si
Gyeonggi-do

01-MAR-2019
KOREA
Galleria West 3F
343 Apgujeong-ro
Gangnam-gu
Seoul
▼

19-MAR-2019
KOREA
Hyundai Daegu 3F
2077 Dalgubeoldae-ro
Jung-gu
Daegu

04-APR-2019
CHINA
Shop 316
Galeries Lafayette
No.110, Beida Street
Xidan, Xicheng District
Beijing

30-AUG-2019
KOREA
Hyundai Sinchon 4F
83 Sinchon-ro
Seodaemun-gu,
Seoul

01-AUG-2019
UAE
Unit L1041, Dubai Mall
Fashion Avenue
Dubai
◀ (left-hand page)

▶

20-SEP-2019
FRANCE
10, rue Clôt Bey
38000 Grenoble

◀
25-SEP-2019
LEBANON
Souks Entertainment Center
Allenby Street
Beirut

30-SEP-2019
KOREA
Hyundai Kintex 2F
817 Hosu-ro Ilsanseo-gu
Gyeonggi-do
Goyang-si

18-OCT-2019
FRANCE
35, rue des Martyrs-de-Vingré
42000 Saint-Étienne

21-NOV-2019
UAE
Unit J29, Level 1
Mall of the Emirates
Dubai

2020 ⎯

◀
09-JAN-2020
LUXEMBOURG
23, rue Philippe-II
2340 Luxembourg

▲
16-JAN-2020
NETHERLANDS
Pieter Cornelisz Hoofstraat 116
1071 Amsterdam

INSPIRATION

"Everything happened as it usually does with us – by chance. Our parents made us take piano lessons. We practiced on a Steinway upright – painful memories of learning to play the classics for four years running, drilled by a female teacher (of course) who seemed alarmingly ancient to us.

But mostly she was so strict that by the time I was ten and Arik was eight we positively hated the exercises in *La Méthode Rose*. Then along came Depeche Mode, Hip Hop and Madonna, and suddenly it was bye-bye dutiful children, bye-bye Schubert's *Trout Quintet* and Mozart's *Turkish March* and hello rock'n'roll. I even wore my mother's oversized perf jacket in an effort to look the part. George Michael, David Bowie – these were the days of

the Walkman and personal cassette players. Of Wednesday afternoons spent at the Virgin Megastore grooving to American soul music. Rhythm and blues, gospel and jazz rolled into one – a sound somewhere between singing and drum, synth and organ. The sound of soul in the style of Marvin Gaye and Nat King Cole. Of Donny Hathaway singing *Everything is Everything*.

Then came the syncopated rhythms of Michael Jackson and *Off the Wall*… and it wasn't long before we were hooked. So what if everything became screechier? Tortured chords; minor chords; semitones; muted instrumentals: the appeal was irresistible. It was one revelation after another. Janis Joplin, Jimi Hendrix, the Beatles, Portishead. Our first Gibson guitar, bought in Pigalle when we were 18. The discovery of another Paris. The Paris of the Bus Palladium, dark songs and a whole new world of uneasy listening.

A first band "Crossman" – memories of a seedy bedroom in a Nolita hotel, alongside the equally seedy recording studios you found in New York in those days. Then it was evening performances at Les Bains Douches, Niel's, The Monkey Club, a studio in the Rue Marbeuf, pretty average but with the feel of 'clean architecture.' Until one night at The Monkey Club –

a performance that turned into a weekly session called 'American Flag' – the sound engineer blew up the PA system after just two numbers …

Music is too important not to be taken seriously. Music lives inside us. It's the score that accompanies a chaotic career, complete with all its ups and downs and everything we communicate through Iro. Middle notes and blues notes for an audience that has embraced us as its own. Thank you to our parents and thank you to Franz Schubert who said: "Always enjoy the present with discernment, so that you may look back fondly on your past and never dread what the future brings."

LB

PLAYLIST

DAVID BOWIE
Heroes

GARY CLARK JUNIOR
Come Together

JIMI HENDRIX
Little Wing

JANIS JOPLIN
Summertime

THE DOORS
People are Strange

LED ZEPPELIN
Stairway to Heaven

NIRVANA
Lithium

EARTH, WIND
AND FIRE
Shining Star

KOOL & THE GANG
Cherish

DEPECHE MODE
Never Let Me Down Again

DONNY HATHAWAY
A Song for You

SERGE GAINSBOURG
Requiem pour un con

THE VELVET
UNDERGROUND
Sunday Morning

PATTI SMITH
Smells Like Teen Spirit

OASIS
Wonderwall

CHARLOTTE
LAWRENCE
Why Do You Love Me

GESAFFELSTEIN
Forever

DEEP DISH
Sergio's Theme

BRODINSKI
Split

SIRIUSMO
Nights Off

PHOTOGRAPHERS

IMAGES

IMMERSION

DAN BALILTY
NEW YORK

ALEXY BENARD
NEW YORK, PARIS, ATELIER, SHOWROOM

INSPIRATION

ACKNOWLEDGEMENTS

We don't believe in vanities, worldliness and empty self-congratulation. For us, walking the tightrope of life is the greatest test of humility. Always in fear of the upcoming season. Certain we can never understand everything. Confident that nothing can be insisted on with certainty. Lucky to be surrounded by great people. We just want to say THANK YOU.

Thank you to the only one without whom there would be nothing. This book tells the story of the thousand crisscrossing paths that have led us to where we are today. A journey made possible by special people who we wish to thank from the bottom of our hearts: Victor and Maguy, Sandy and Johana, Anthony and Illana. Erin, Chloé, Ron, Liv, Jude, Yeoudite, Levin, Aaron, Abigail, Iska and Yanai. Rahav Zuta and Chloé Millier who we grew up with. Not forgetting all of those who have helped Iro to blossom over the past 15 years. Thank you to Allan Xia and Liu Sujuan for believing in us.

Thank you to the teams at Studio, to the atelier team, the production team, the marketing communications team, the merchandising team, the global design team, the network team, the logistics team, the distribution team and the software and e-commerce development teams. Thank you to Accounting, Human Resources and General Services. Thank you to our boutique staff in Paris, France and the rest of Europe, in the USA and in China. Thank you to our suppliers, to our wholesale customers across the globe, to our distributors, agents and representatives. Thank you to the French and international press for their invaluable support. And above all, a big thank-you to our *clientes*: all of those women and girls who embody our dreams.

Our thanks also to everyone who had a hand in this book. To photographers Benoît Peverelli, Chris Colls, Claudia Knoepfel and Stefan Indlekofer, Collier Schorr, Josh Olins, Karim Sadli, Lachlan Bailey and to Alexy Benard and Dan Balilty for the immersive images. To models such as Abbey Lee Kershaw, Altyn Simpson, Anja Rubik, Aymeline Valade, Constance Jablonski, Edita Vilkeviciute, Eniko Mihalik, Karlie Kloss, Karmen Pedaru, Kasia Struss, Kati Nescher, Lexi Boling, Luna Bijl, Magdalena Frackowiak, Sasha Pivovarova and Taylor Hill. To the agencies who supported us: Elite, Ford, IMG, Metropolitan, Next, Viva, Women, etc. And to stylists Clare Richardson, Géraldine Saglio, Haley Wollens, Mélanie Huynh, Véronique Didry and Virginie Benarroch.

Thank you too to Aude Perrier, Virginie Heid, Corinne Schmidt, Virginie Mahieux, John Briens, Alexy Benard, Chloé Marchi and Valérie-Anne Diot. To Flo Brutton for the translation. This book has been a fantastic experience that will remain forever in our memories.

A heartfelt thank you to Laurence Benaïm for agreeing to take part in a project that was so dear to our hearts. Ours was a special meeting, not least because it provided a foretaste of those shared and deeply moving moments in store. All of them rooted in honesty, humility and the affection forged between us. Laurence found just the right words to describe our experience of life. Words steeped in sincerity from beginning to end. Words that flowed from her magical pen to give concrete expression to the things we had only imagined. We very much hope she will use that pen again on behalf of the other projects we have in the pipeline…

Thank you to the music that is a constant in our lives. The music to which we owe so much and that one day we fully intend to repay.

Arik and Laurent Bitton

PHOTO CREDITS

© LACHLAN BAILEY / Art Partner: 110-117
© CHRIS COLLS: 50-65,164-177
© CLAUDIA KNOEPFEL AND STEFAN INDLEKOFER: 14-21, 30-35, 72-79, 80-83, 84-87
© JOSH OLINS: first cover, 9, 146-157
© BENOÎT PEVERELLI: 158-163
© KARIM SADLI / Art + Commerce: 22-29
© COLLIER SCHORR: 36-49, 66-71, 88-99, 100-109, 118-129, 130-138, 140-144

IMMERSION
© DAN BALILTY: New York
© ALEXY BENARD: New York, Paris, Studio, Showroom

INSPIRATION
© ALEXY BENARD: 222-223

INVITATION
© Tanju Özelgin Studio: 215, 216-217, 219

Graphic design and production: avecbrio.fr
Publishing: Virginie Mahieux

Texts: Laurence Benaïm

Translation and proofreading: Flo Brutton

Copyright ©2020, Éditions de La Martinière, an imprint of EDLM
for the original and English translation
10 9 8 7 6 5 4 3 2 1

Abrams books are available at special discounts when purchased in quantity
for premiums and promotions as well as fundraising or educational use.
Special editions can also be created to specification. For details,
contact specialsales@abramsbooks.com or the address below.

Photoengraving: Escourbiac
Printed and bound in March 2020 by Escourbiac
ISBN: 9781419750731
Legal Deposit: March 2020
10 9 8 7 6 5 4 3 2 1
Printed in France

195 Broadway
New York, NY 10007
ABRAMS   abramsbooks.com